Famous Trials

GLEN DOWNEY

Editorial Board
David Booth • Joan Green • Jack Booth

HOUGHTON MIFFLIN HARCOURT

10801 N. Mopac Expressway
Building # 3
Austin, TX 78759
1.800.531.5015

Steck-Vaughn is a trademark of HMH Supplemental Publishers Inc. registered in the United States of America and/or other jurisdictions. All inquiries should be mailed to HMH Supplemental Publishers Inc., P.O. Box 27010, Austin, TX 78755.

www.rubiconpublishing.com

Copyright © 2006 Rubicon Publishing Inc. Published by Rubicon Publishing Inc. All rights reserved. No part of this publication may be reproduced or transmitted in any form or by any means, electronic or mechanical, including photocopying, recording, taping, or any information storage and retrieval system, without the prior written permission of the copyright holder unless such copying is expressly permitted by federal copyright law.

Project Editors: Miriam Bardswich, Kim Koh
Editor: Julie Flannery
Editorial Assistant: Kermin Bhot
Art/Creative Director: Jennifer Drew
Assistant Art Director: Jen Harvey
Designer: Jeanette Debusschere
Cover images–iStockphoto; title page–Junial Enterprises/Shutterstock.com

Printed in Singapore

ISBN: 978-1-419-02450-4
2 3 4 5 6 7 8 9 10 11   2015   24 23 22 21 20 19 18 17 16 15
A B C D E F G

If you have received these materials as examination copies free of charge, Houghton Mifflin Harcourt Publishing Company retains title to the materials and they may not be resold. Resale of examination copies is strictly prohibited.

Possession of this publication in print format does not entitle users to convert this publication, or any portion of it, into electronic format.

CONTENTS

4 Introduction: What Makes a Trial Famous?

6 Trial By Ordeal
Check out these explanations of how it was decided if a person was guilty or innocent back in the Middle Ages.

8 Off With Their Heads!
Historical accounts of how some kings lost their heads — literally.

10 The Monkey Trial
In this excerpt of a transcript from the famous Scopes Trial, defense lawyer Clarence Darrow asks the jury to find his client guilty! Find out why.

16 Train Ride to Prison
Read the true account of the Scottsboro boys, and how their story inspired the famous novel *To Kill a Mockingbird*.

20 The Trial of the 20th Century
A report about the end of World War II when some of the most notorious members of the Nazi Party were tried for crimes in the infamous Nuremberg trials.

24 Too Young to Die
In 1959, 12-year-old Lynne Harper was murdered. This newspaper report tells how her 14-year-old friend was accused.

28 27 Years to Freedom
Nelson Mandela spent nearly three decades in prison. This excerpt is from a famous statement he made in court during his 1964 trial.

32 Jack Ruby
In this graphic story, Jack Ruby avenges the president's death by taking matters into his own hands.

36 From Heiress to Terrorist
Patty Hearst was an heiress to millions. Then one day, she was kidnapped, brainwashed, and became a bank-robbing terrorist. Read this true account.

40 To Whom It May Concern
Read excerpts from O.J.'s actual "suicide letter," written just five days after the murders of his ex-wife and her close friend.

42 When Children Kill
Two-year-old James Bulger was beaten to death … by two 10-year-old boys. Find out what happened in this report of their murder trial.

45 Woman Exposes Corporation
A true account of the real Erin Brockovich and how her courage and dedication scored one for the little guy.

What Makes a Trial Famous?

Ladies and gentlemen of the jury, this book begins by asking you an important question: What makes a trial famous?

Sometimes a famous trial has a well-known defendant, sometimes the crime is unusually shocking, and sometimes one of the attorneys is so good, or so bad, that he or she determines the outcome. And then there are trials in which all of these things are true. These trials usually become so famous that we talk about them long after they have come and gone. This is especially true when we feel that the jury's verdict in the case was incorrect.

This book looks at some of the most famous trials in history. Whether or not these trials are still famous 50 or 100 years from now will depend on you. Like the members of a jury, you have to make the decision. Think carefully, ladies and gentlemen, before you reach your verdict!

TRIAL BY ORDEAL

warm up

Have you ever seen movies or television programs of trials during medieval times? What were they like? Share your thoughts with the class.

Court trials today are organized proceedings with prosecuting attorneys and defense lawyers, fair judges and responsible juries, and the right of defendants to choose counsel and to decide whether or not they will take the stand. Before Trial by Jury, there was Trial by Ordeal, in which the guilt or innocence of defendants was determined by putting them in physical danger and seeing what happened to them. Two of the most common were Trial by Water and Trial by Fire.

proceedings: *events*

FYI

Another form of trial in the Middle Ages was Trial by Battle, in which two individuals would duel each other until one was dead or injured. The judgment of the case would go in favor of the person who won the duel.

CHECKPOINT

What problems can you see with this method of putting someone on trial?

TRIAL BY WATER

This usually involved:

1. Having the accused remove an object from a pot of boiling liquid. If the accused was unharmed after removing the object, he or she was declared innocent.

2. Making the accused drink "bitter" or poisoned water. If the authorities wanted to find a person guilty, all they needed to do was provide a strong enough dose of poison!

3. Throwing the accused into water with a weight tied around him or her. Religious leaders of the day believed that if the accused sank, he or she was innocent. If the accused floated, he or she was thought to possess supernatural powers and was declared guilty.

CHECKPOINT
Notice how an accused person did not have any rights and could be doomed no matter what happened.

TRIAL BY FIRE

The accused person was forced to walk nine paces across flaming metal or carry a red hot metal rod in his or her hands. If the person was uninjured, he or she was innocent. If the person was screaming in agony from second and third degree burns, as was more likely the case, he or she was guilty. In some cases, the burning was not judged to be important, only how the wounds healed. Quick healing showed that the person was innocent while sores and infection revealed that the person was guilty.

wrap up
Imagine that you are living during the Middle Ages. Prepare a short speech in which you argue that a Trial by Ordeal that you witnessed could not possibly determine a person's guilt or innocence.

WEB CONNECTIONS
Use the Internet to research trials in the Middle Ages. What methods, in addition to those mentioned here, were used? Report your findings to the class.

Off with Their Heads!

LOUIS XVI (1792-93)

warm up

Have you ever been accused of something and found it difficult to defend yourself? With a partner, discuss what happened and how you dealt with it.

CHECKPOINT

What might the difficulties be of having this kind of jury system today?

###

The guillotine is named for its French inventor, Dr. Joseph Ignace Guillotin, who wanted a more humane means of executing criminals. He hoped that one day, capital punishment (the death penalty) would be abolished.

The trial of Louis XVI took place during the French Revolution. Angered that the king had wasted the country's money and had done nothing for the poor, the common people of France rose up and overthrew him. Louis was finally arrested and put on trial for treason. However, the trial was quite different from jury trials today. Instead of 12 men and women deciding Louis' fate, there were more than 700 men who sat in judgment of him. Decisions were made by a majority of votes.

The trial also proceeded differently from modern trials. The person who presided over the trial read the charges against Louis, which included making the army march against the citizens of Paris, not upholding the constitution, and destroying the French navy. He then questioned Louis for more than two hours. Louis' defense was that he was the king, and did not have to do things differently from what he had done. For hundreds of years the king's rule had been absolute. This was not a very popular defense because it was this sort of power that the people who supported the revolution objected to.

presided over: *supervised*   upholding: *supporting*

His lawyers argued that Louis XVI had followed the country's constitution, and that he was now being unfairly tried under laws that did not exist when he was king. They made a good case, but the revolutionaries were determined to find him guilty.

When the proceedings were over, the Convention, the law-making body during the French Revolution, voted and 693 members said that Louis was guilty of conspiring against France and threatening its safety. A motion to let the common people decide his fate was rejected. The last vote taken decided whether Louis should be executed. The Convention voted 383 to 334 in favor of death. On January 21, 1793, Louis XVI was led to the guillotine and beheaded.

CHECKPOINT
Do you think Louis XVI should have tried to come up with a different strategy for his defense?

WEB CONNECTIONS
Marie Antoinette, the wife of Louis XVI, was well known for her disdain for the common people. Use the Internet to find out what she was charged with, when her trial took place, and what the verdict was. Report your findings to the class.

wrap up
1. Make a list of the similarities you see between the cases of Louis XVI and Charles I. Share your list with the class.

2. With a partner, design a poster that could have been displayed in Paris during the trial of Louis XVI. Your poster should either ask for Louis to be set free or sent to the guillotine.

CHARLES I (1649)

Although Charles I was the King of England, he could not stop a revolution led by Oliver Cromwell and the Roundheads, a group of Englishmen who supported Parliament rather than the king. Angry at the king's contempt for Parliament, they overthrew Charles and put him on trial as a traitor, tyrant, and murderer. Charles refused to acknowledge that anyone could put him on trial, but the panel of judges convicted him. When he finally tried to speak in his own defense he was told he was too late. His date of execution was set for January 30, 1649, when he was beheaded.

contempt: *disobedience and disrespect*

The Monkey Trial

JOHN THOMAS SCOPES (1925)

warm up

What limits, if any, should the courts place on what teachers are allowed to teach in their classrooms? Share your ideas with the rest of the class.

CHECKPOINT

Why do you think that the trial came to be known by this name?

John Thomas Scopes was a schoolteacher in Tennessee who taught his class about the Theory of Evolution, the idea that human beings were not created by a god, but evolved from animals like apes. However, in Tennessee at that time, an anti-evolution *statute* held that teaching evolution was illegal and punishable by up to a $500 fine.

When Scopes was arrested and charged, the case drew the attention of two of the most famous lawyers of the day, William Jennings Bryan for the prosecution, and Clarence Darrow for the defense. Bryan and Darrow engaged in one of the most famous courtroom battles of all time in what came to be known as the Scopes Monkey Trial.

Darrow did not deny that his client, John Thomas Scopes, taught evolution. He argued that the issue of freedom of speech was important enough that he was willing to take the case all the way to the Supreme Court. In the following excerpt, Darrow asks the jury to find his client guilty so that he can appeal the case to a higher court!

statute: law

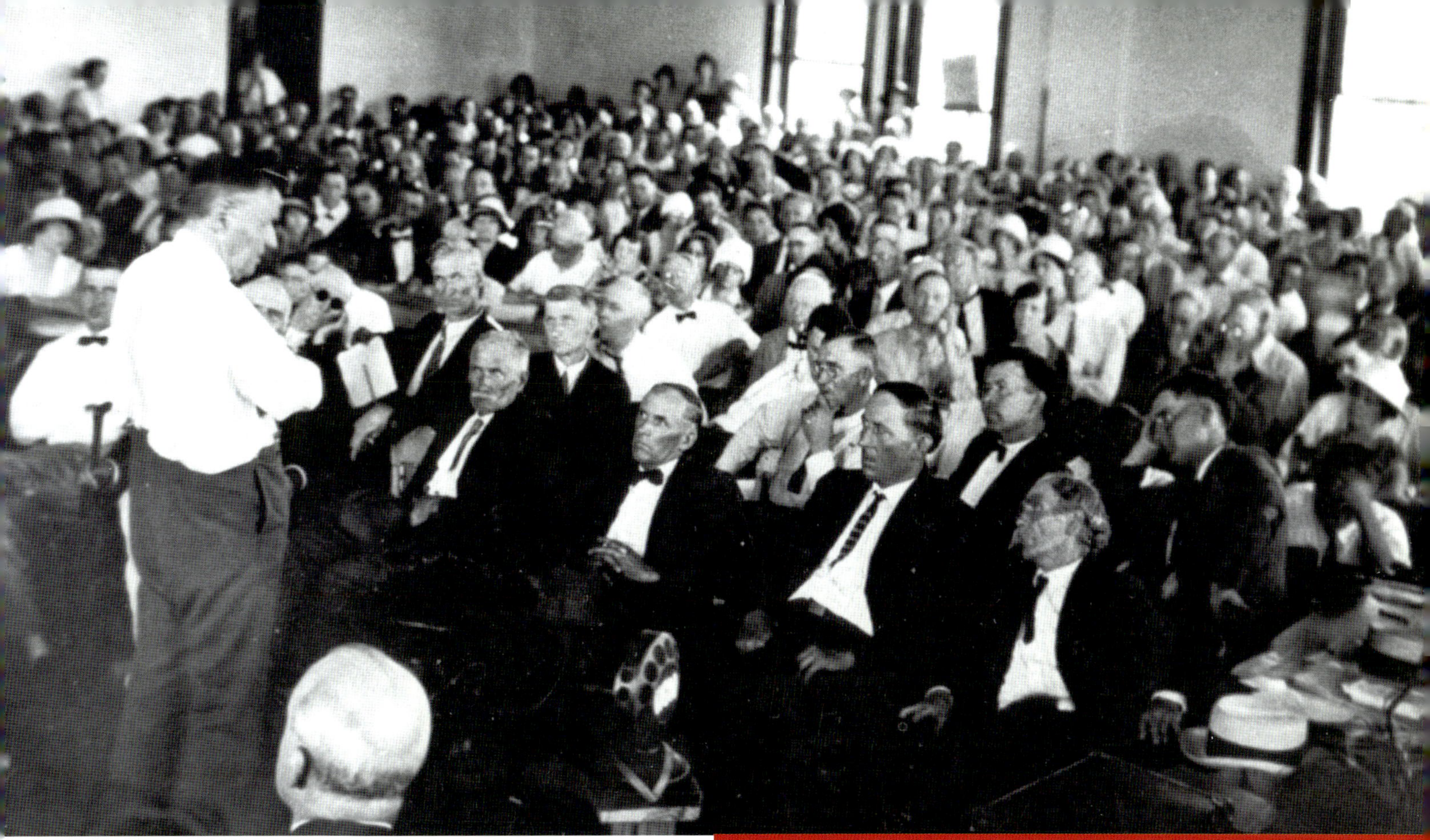

Clarence Darrow addresses the jury.

DARROW: ... The court has told you very plainly that if you think my client taught that man descended from a lower order of animals, you will find him guilty, and you heard the testimony ... and there is no dispute about the facts.

I do not know how you may feel, I am not especially interested in it, but this case and this law will never be decided until it gets to a higher court, and it cannot get to a higher court probably, very well, unless you bring in a verdict. So, I do not want any of you to think we are going to find any fault with you as to your verdict.

CHECKPOINT

Notice how Darrow has bigger plans for this issue.

I am frank to say, while we think it is wrong, and we ought to have been permitted to put in our evidence, the court felt otherwise ... We cannot argue to you gentlemen under the instructions given by the court — we cannot even explain to you that we think

John Scopes and Clarence Darrow

Evolution–tsaplia/Shutterstock.com; Scopes Trial Photos–Bryan College Archives

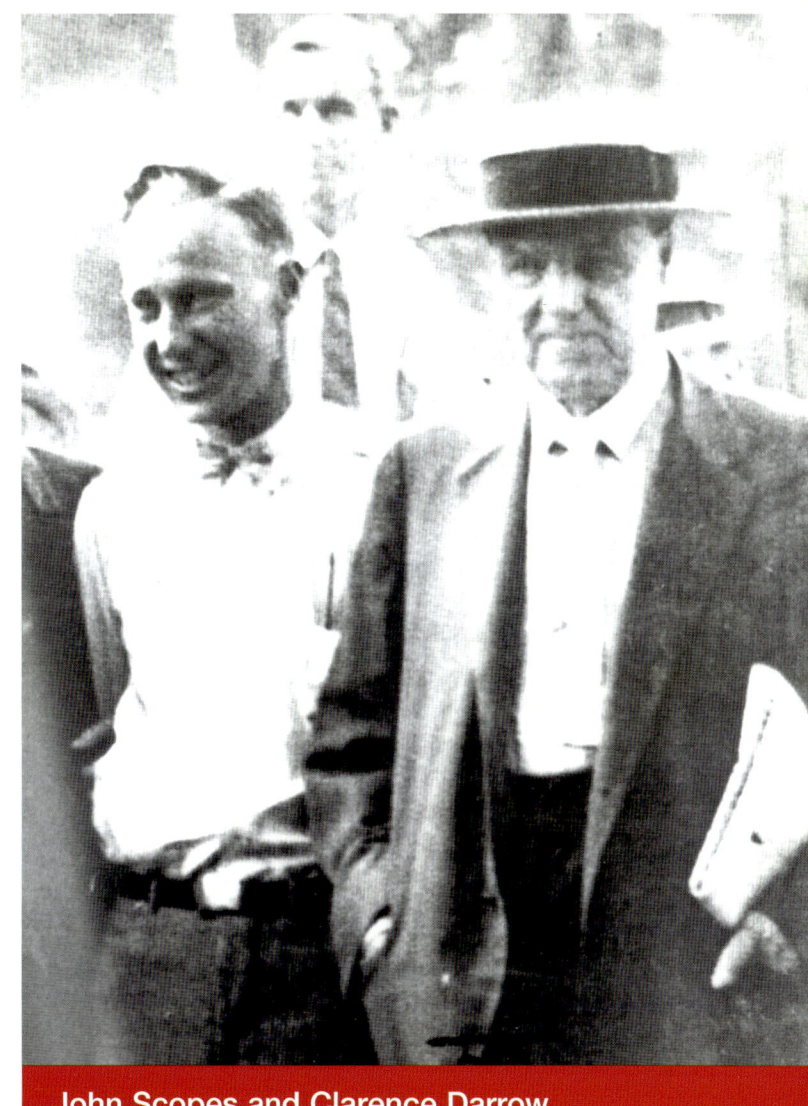

William Jennings Bryan addresses the court.

you should return a verdict of not guilty ... We think we will save our point and take it to the higher court and settle whether the law is good, and also whether he should have permitted the evidence. I guess that is plain enough.

> **CHECKPOINT**
>
> Notice that Darrow is basically asking the jury to find his client guilty.

After this plea by Clarence Darrow to find his client guilty so the case could be appealed, the verdict was not a surprise.

COURT: Mr. Foreman, will you tell us whether you have agreed on a verdict?

FOREMAN: Yes, sir, we have, Your Honor.

COURT: What do you find?

FOREMAN: We have found for the state — found the defendant guilty.

COURT: Did you fix the fine?

FOREMAN: No, sir.

COURT: You leave it to the court?

FOREMAN: Leave it to the court.

COURT: Mr. Scopes, will you come around here, please, sir. (The defendant presents himself before the court.)

Mr. Scopes, the jury has found you guilty under this indictment, charging you with having taught in the schools of Rhea County, in violation of what is commonly known as the anti-evolution statute, which makes it unlawful for any teacher to teach in any of the public schools of the state ...

---

indictment: *particular charge*

any theory that denies the story of the divine creation of man, and teach instead thereof that man has descended from a lower order of animals. The jury has found you guilty. The statute makes this an offense punishable by a fine of not less than $100 or more than $500. The court now fixes your fine at $100 and imposes that fine upon you.

Oh, have you anything to say, Mr. Scopes, as to why the court should not impose punishment upon you?

DEFENDANT J.T. SCOPES: Your Honor, I feel that I have been convicted of violating an unjust statute. I will continue in the future, as I have in the past, to oppose this law in any way I can. Any other action would be in violation of my ideal of academic freedom — that is, to teach the truth as guaranteed in our constitution of personal and religious freedom. I think the fine is unjust.

The verdict went against Scopes but the outcome of the trial was really a victory for the defense. Attention from all over the world had been drawn to the case and the fine was thrown out on a technicality.

divine creation of man: *created by God*

technicality: *a detail that is considered insignificant*

John Scopes is sentenced at the conclusion of the trial.

Gathering Data for the Tennessee Trial

The Scopes trial did not go beyond Tennessee but the evolution versus creation, science versus religion debate raged on in the United States.

Creationism on Trial

EPPERSON V. ARKANSAS (1968)

Since the Scopes trial, there have been several cases in the United States in which creationism has been put on trial. One of the most famous was the case of Susan Epperson, a high school biology teacher who volunteered to challenge an Arkansas law that prevented her from teaching evolution in her grade 10 biology class. The United States Supreme Court ultimately decided that the law prohibiting the teaching of evolution was unconstitutional since states are not allowed to require teaching based on religious principles or prohibitions.

unconstitutional: *unlawful*
prohibitions: *bans*

FYI

In 1925, Tennessee passed the Butler Act, the law prohibiting the teaching of evolution in public schools. On May 17, 1967, Tennessee withdrew this act.

CHECKPOINT

Why do you think the constitution would want to prevent states from doing this?

EDWARDS V. AGUILLARD (1987)

In 1982, Louisiana passed a Balanced Treatment Act that prevented the teaching of evolution unless it included instruction in creation science. However, parents, teachers, and religious leaders challenged the act because they believed that the state was endorsing religion and establishing it in public schools. The Supreme Court ruled that the act was unconstitutional, finding that it served a religious purpose: it supported religious teachings by preventing evolution from being taught unless a religious perspective of that subject was presented with it. The court ruled that the act violated the First Amendment of the United States Constitution, and declared that "forbidding the teaching of evolution when creation science is not also taught undermines the provision of a comprehensive scientific education."

endorsing: *supporting*

FYI

Edwin W. Edwards was the governor of Louisiana and Donald Aguillard represented the teachers and parents.

wrap up

1. Review the excerpt from Darrow's speech and summarize in one well-developed paragraph what you find effective about it.

2. Make a list of three questions that you would like to ask one of the participants in the three trials featured in this article. Share your questions with a small group.

3. Explain why the cartoon, "Gathering Data for the Tennessee Trial," is or is not effective in getting its message across.

TRAIN RIDE TO PRISON

SCOTTSBORO BOYS (1931-37)

warm up

Have you ever been falsely accused of something? Describe the situation to the class and explain what you did about it.

During the Depression, jobs were scarce. People looking for temporary work traveled across the country by hopping onto boxcars. On March 25, 1931, on a train from Chattanooga to Memphis, Tennessee, there was a confrontation between two groups of youths — one white and the other African American. After the black youths threw some of the white youths off the train, the white youths told local authorities about the incident. As a result, nine young black men were arrested as the train pulled into Paint Rock, Alabama. Two young white women, Victoria Price and Ruby Bates, who were also on the train, then accused the black youths of raping them. Although they were lying in order to avoid getting in trouble for illegally hitching a ride on the train, the women's story was immediately believed and all nine youths were charged with assault and rape.

CHECKPOINT

Why do you think the women's story was believed immediately?

Within two weeks' time, eight of the nine boys were tried, convicted, and sentenced to death in the electric chair. The trial of Roy Wright was declared a mistrial because several jury members wanted to hold out for the death penalty even though the prosecutor asked that they only sentence the defendant to life imprisonment.

confrontation: *argument*

Defense attorney Samuel Leibowitz meets his clients; Scottsboro, Alabama (1933).

In 2003, Atticus Finch was rated the top movie hero in the American Film Institute's list of 100 movie heroes.

CHECKPOINT

If Ruby Bates finally admitted that the story was made up, why do you think the Scottsboro boys were not released from prison right away?

FYI

The nine Scottsboro boys were Clarence Norris, Charlie Weems, Haywood Patterson, Olen Montgomery, Ozie Powell, Willie Roberson, Eugene Williams, Andy Wright, and Roy Wright.

The case of the Scottsboro boys helped to ignite the Civil Rights movement of the 1960s — a movement that saw the desegregation of schools and increased rights for African Americans.

What no one could have known about this apparently open-and-shut case was that the U.S. Supreme Court would overturn the original convictions in November of 1932. Over the next several years there were a series of trials and retrials. The boys were repeatedly convicted, sentenced to death, and had their sentences upheld by the Alabama Supreme Court only to have them overturned by the U.S. Supreme Court. Ruby Bates later admitted that the whole story had been made up, but this did not prevent the Scottsboro boys from spending many years in jail. It was not until 1950 that the last of the men was paroled, and not until 1976 that the governor of Alabama pardoned Clarence Norris, the last surviving Scottsboro boy.

This case was important for it showed not only the problems of racism in the American South, but how the justice system needed to change by respecting the rights of black defendants and allowing African Americans to sit on juries.

Gregory Peck is shown as attorney Atticus Finch in a scene from the 1962 movie *To Kill a Mockingbird*.

The idea of a black man being falsely accused of raping a white woman made its way into one of the most famous American novels of the 20th century: Harper Lee's *To Kill a Mockingbird*. The novel takes place in the small Alabama town of Maycomb where a white lawyer named Atticus Finch defends a black man, Tom Robinson, who has been accused of raping a white woman. Atticus, an upright lawyer with strong ethics, makes a noble effort to overcome the racism of his community in defending his client.

When Atticus decides to take on Tom's case, several of the townspeople turn against him. Bob Ewell, the racist father of the so-called victim, becomes his biggest opponent. For Atticus, unlike many inhabitants of Maycomb, Tom's situation is about justice and not skin color. At the time, things are changing slowly in the South and there are many more men like Bob Ewell in Maycomb who see black men as frightening figures.

In his most famous speech in the novel, Atticus explains that the townspeople make assumptions about their black neighbors and believe "that *all* Negroes lie, that *all* Negroes are basically immoral beings, that *all* Negro men are not to be trusted around women …".

Atticus Finch presents a very strong case that proves that Tom Robinson did not commit the crime. However, the jury is unwilling to accept the word of a black man over that of a white one and finds the charged man guilty. Justice is not served, and tragedy results.

---

ethics: *morals*

CHECKPOINT
Think of how difficult it would be to ensure a fair trial under these circumstances.

wrap up

1. Refer to the photograph on page 17 and make a list of seven descriptive words that convey the mood in this picture. Indicate which word refers to whom or what. Share your list with a partner.

2. Imagine you've been asked to obtain signatures on a petition to free the Scottsboro boys. With a partner, discuss how you would convince people to sign your petition.

WEB CONNECTIONS

Search the Internet to find the two best websites dealing with the Scottsboro Trials. Defend your choices by preparing notes on the features of each of the sites.

The Trial of the 20th Century
NUREMBERG TRIALS (1945-46)

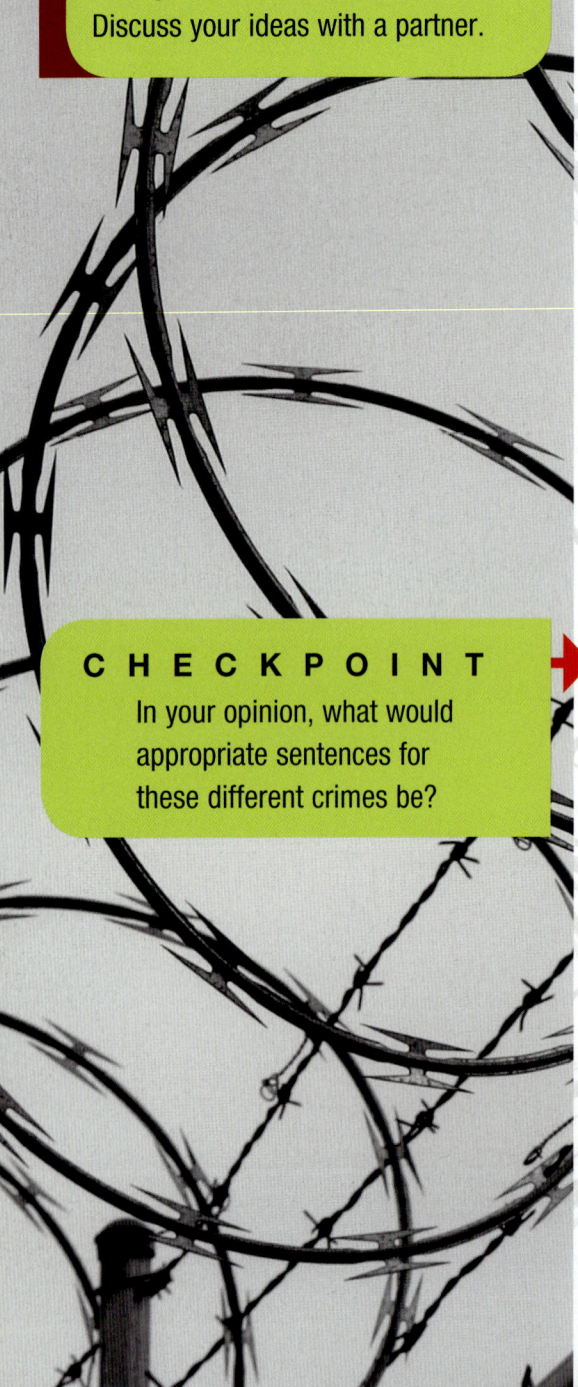

warm up
How should government and military leaders who commit serious crimes during wartime be dealt with? Discuss your ideas with a partner.

CHECKPOINT
In your opinion, what would appropriate sentences for these different crimes be?

At the end of World War II, the governments of the United States, Great Britain, France, and the Soviet Union established the International Military Tribunal in order to prosecute members of the Nazi party who committed serious crimes. In total, 12 trials took place from 1945 to 1949. Most of the attention focused on the first trial in which 21 defendants were tried by this international court in Nuremberg, Germany. These included such infamous Nazis as Hermann Goering and Rudolf Hess.

The following charges were laid against the accused:

- "Crimes against peace" included preparing and planning to wage aggressive war and waging aggressive war.

- "War crimes" included murder, ill treatment or deportation of prisoners, killing of hostages, plundering public and private property, unnecessary destruction of cities, towns, and villages, or other devastation not necessary for military purposes.

- "Crimes against humanity" included murder, extermination, enslavement, deportation, and other inhumane acts committed against civilians, which included the killing of more than six million Jewish people in death and concentration camps.

The Nuremberg trials involved a cast of hundreds and perhaps thousands. Legal workers in huge numbers were engaged in either preparing for the prosecution or defense of the accused. Thousands of documents were captured and reviewed as potential evidence in the trials. Members of the world press took over the major hotel in Nuremberg and nearly a thousand workers completed the restoration of the Palace of Justice where the trials were held.

When the first trial was over, 18 defendants were sentenced and three were acquitted. Eleven were sentenced to death by hanging and seven were given prison terms ranging from 10 years to life.

---

infamous: *well-known for evil acts*
deportation: *forced exile*
plundering: *robbing*
enslavement: *the act of taking away all freedom*

◀ The International Military Tribunal at the opening session of the trial of war criminals at Nuremberg on November 20, 1945.

▲ The defendants and their lawyers hear the reading of the charges on the first day of the trial on November 20, 1945.

▲ A tank guards the entrance to the Palace of Justice in Nuremberg, where the International Military Tribunal trial was held.

▲ American army staffers organize stacks of German documents that were collected by war crimes investigators as evidence for the trials.

◀ Aerial view of the Nuremberg prison, where the defendants were held.

▼ The photo below shows the main cell block in the Nuremberg prison, where defendants standing trial were held. One guard was posted at the entrance of each prisoner's cell in order to prevent suicide attempts.

▲ Alfred Rosenberg, a former Nazi Party official, in the witness box at Nuremberg. Rosenberg was convicted of war crimes and crimes against humanity and hanged in October 1946.

▲ Defendant Hermann Goering consults with his lawyer, Dr. Otto Stahmer, in the Nuremberg prison. Goering was the Commander-in-Chief of the *Luftwaffe*, the German air force. He was sentenced to death for his crimes but just two hours before his execution, he committed suicide by swallowing a capsule of poison that he managed to smuggle into prison.

◂ A crowd eagerly reads the special edition of the Nuremberg newspaper reporting on the sentences handed out by the International Military Tribunal on October 1, 1946.

Nuremberg saw 11 additional trials of Nazi defendants by various tribunals between 1946 and 1949. Nazi doctors who worked at the death camps and performed horrifying experiments on inmates were tried, convicted, and sentenced to imprisonment or death. So were members of the *Einsatzgruppen*, squads of armed military personnel who were responsible for murdering thousands and burying them in mass graves. The courts also tried various Nazi ministers, judges, and others guilty of war crimes and crimes against humanity during this time.

▴ Defendant Oswald Pohl, a major leader in Hitler's former police force, is sentenced to death by the Military Tribunal II. He was executed on June 8, 1951.

▴ Defendant Paul Blobel is sentenced to death at another of the subsequent trials. He was hanged on June 8, 1951.

FYI

Rudolph Hess, a top Nazi official, spent more than 40 years as an inmate of Spandau Prison. From 1966 until his suicide in 1987, Hess was Spandau's only inmate.

wrap up

1. Working in a small group, make a list of things shown in the photographs which show that the Nuremberg trials were very important.

2. Many of the Nazi defendants at Nuremberg argued that they were just carrying out orders given to them by their superiors. In a paragraph, explain whether or not that should be considered as an explanation when dealing with such serious crimes.

Too Young

STEVEN TRUSCOTT (1959)

warm up

Do you think that capital punishment (the death penalty) is an appropriate punishment for certain crimes? Discuss this issue with a partner.

On June 9, 1959, a 12-year-old girl, Lynne Harper, was sexually assaulted and strangled in Clinton, Ontario. One of her classmates, 14-year-old Steven Truscott, was taken into police custody and charged with these crimes on June 12, 1959, just one day after her body was found. The case was built on purely circumstantial evidence and rested on the testimony of the pathologist who gave a very specific time of death, the accuracy of which was questionable.

CHECKPOINT
Does this seem like a reasonable amount of time to check all the evidence?

Steven was ordered to stand trial in adult court despite his young age. The trial began on September 16, 1959, and was over after a mere two weeks. Although the evidence against him was questionable, both the prosecutor and the judge were convinced of his guilt.

It is now believed that the police laid charges too quickly while ignoring other possible suspects and playing down some witnesses. As well, Judge Ferguson may have influenced the outcome of the trial. In his charge to the jury, he drew their attention to the major evidence presented by the prosecution without giving equal time to the evidence presented by the defense.

CHECKPOINT
Compare the length of this trial to the length of murder trials today.

circumstantial evidence: *evidence that does not directly relate to the facts*
pathologist: *medical examiner*

to Die

After a six-hour deliberation, the jury found Steven Truscott guilty but asked for mercy in his sentence.

However, Judge Ferguson ignored the plea for mercy. He sentenced Steven to be executed on December 8, 1959, and stated that on that day "… you be taken to the place of execution, and that you there be hanged by the neck until you are dead …".

It is not surprising that Steven was found guilty given the media attention the case received. The headlines from 1959 left little doubt in the minds of readers that an offender had to be found, and found quickly.

Steven Truscott's sentence was eventually commuted to life imprisonment and he was released from prison on parole in 1969. He married, had three children, and began a new life. Truscott has recently come into the public spotlight once again in an effort to finally clear his name. The following excerpt from the Calgary Herald *outlines these recent efforts.*

---

deliberation: *discussion before making a decision*
commuted: *changed the penalty to a less severe form*

Truscott hopes for final exoneration

By Janice Tibbetts
April 15, 2004

The fate of Steven Truscott, convicted of one of the most notorious murders in Canadian history, rests in a hefty report of about 800 pages that a judge is expected to deliver within days to Justice Minister Irwin Cotler.

Now a 59-year-old father of three, Truscott's dream is to return to the courthouse in Goderich, Ont., where he was sentenced to death for the murder of his schoolmate 45 years ago — and this time he wants to walk away exonerated.

"He wants to go into the very courtroom where he was convicted and sentenced to death," said his lawyer, James Lockyer.

> **CHECKPOINT**
> Why do you think this is so important to Truscott?

"He wants to have the attorney general of Ontario acknowledge that he didn't commit the crime."

Retired justice Fred Kaufman was asked two years ago by then Justice Minister Martin Cauchon to review whether Truscott was wrongly convicted of strangling his 12-year-old classmate, Lynne Harper, on a June evening in 1959 near a Canadian military base outside Clinton, Ont.

Truscott found himself at the center of one of Canada's most sensational murder trials after giving Harper a lift on his bicycle down a country road near a popular swimming hole.

He was the last known person to see the girl alive.

At age 14, he became the youngest Canadian ever sent to death row, but his sentence was commuted to life imprisonment and he was released on parole in 1969 …

Kaufman, a former Quebec Court of Appeal justice … will make a recommendation to Cotler in his expansive report …

The Toronto-based Association in Defence of the Wrongly Convicted pressured the federal government into reviewing the case more than two years ago under a seldom-used Criminal Code provision that remedies miscarriages of justice …

---

notorious: *known for unfavorable reasons*
exonerated: *cleared*

On October 28, 2004, Justice Minister Irwin Cotler stated, "I have determined there is a reasonable basis to conclude that a miscarriage of justice likely occurred in this case." He decided to forward the matter to the Ontario Court of Appeal for a final decision. This was seen by many as a compromise between rejecting Truscott's wrongful conviction claim and ordering a new trial. Although the family was very upset by this compromise decision, Truscott himself put it into perspective: "It's a bump on the road," he told The Globe and Mail. "Once they sentence you to hang, what else can they do to you?"

Steven Truscott's wife, Marlene, rests her head on his shoulder as they listen to his lawyers speak outside their family home, October 28, 2004.

FYI

The last execution in Canada took place in 1962. In 1976, the passing of Bill C-84 outlawed capital punishment for any crime.

In Steven Truscott's fight to clear his name, he has been helped by Rubin "Hurricane" Carter, a former prize-fighter from the United States who spent many years in prison for a crime he did not commit.

wrap up

1. Working with a partner, search for evidence in the article that indicates Steven Truscott may not have received a fair trial in September 1959. Make a list of your findings.

2. Write a letter to the editor of your local newspaper expressing your opinion on Justice Minister Cotler's recent decision.

WEB CONNECTIONS

Use the Internet to research what evidence may have been ignored by the police and prosecution at Steven Truscott's trial in 1959. Share your findings with the class.

27 Years to Freedom

NELSON MANDELA (1964)

warm up

Is a criminal act always wrong, or are there certain instances in which committing a crime might be valid or even necessary? Share your opinion with the rest of the class.

CHECKPOINT

Do you feel that such action on the part of Mandela and others can be justified?

Before Nelson Mandela won the Nobel Prize for Peace and served as President of South Africa, he spent nearly three decades in prison because of the threat he posed to South Africa's ruling white minority. Fed up with the fact that peaceful demonstrations by black South Africans were being ignored, Mandela co-founded a wing of the African National Congress (ANC) that *advocated* the use of force. He and others began a campaign of *sabotage* against military and government targets, and were prepared to take this further if they could not stop the oppression of their people.

In 1962, Nelson Mandela was arrested for traveling abroad and *inciting* workers to strike — things he was expressly forbidden to do. While serving his five-year prison sentence, he was charged with sabotage and treason when some of his fellow ANC members were arrested. He was tried for these crimes, at the now infamous Rivonia Trial of 1964, was convicted, and sentenced to life imprisonment. The following excerpt is from the famous statement Mandela made to the members of the court on April 20, 1964. In it, he sums up the frustration of black South Africans living in a racist society.

advocated: promoted or supported
sabotage: deliberate damage
inciting: encouraging

In 1994, Nelson Mandela visits the cell in Robben Island Prison where he was held as a political prisoner by the apartheid-based government from 1964 to 1990 for sabotage.

apartheid: *South African policy to separate people according to color*

NELSON MANDELA
A symbol of courage and resistance of the South African oppressed people. 1987 marks 25 years of his imprisonment by the racist Pretoria regime.

Awarded the freedom of the CITY of SYDNEY and the GEORGI DIMITROV ORDER, the highest honour given by the People's Republic of Bulgaria to international freedom fighters, at celebrations commemorating the 75th Anniversary of the African National Congress.
FIGHT FOR HIS RELEASE AND THAT OF ALL SOUTH AFRICAN POLITICAL PRISONERS

FYI

Mandela and many others were arrested first in 1956 and put on trial for treason (because of their political activities), but all of the defendants in this case were eventually acquitted.

In 2001, Nelson Mandela received the Order of Canada and was made an honorary Canadian citizen, only the second non-Canadian to receive this honor.

"Africans want to be paid a living wage. Africans want to perform work, which they are capable of doing, and not work which the Government declares them to be capable of. Africans want to be allowed to live where they obtain work, and not be endorsed out of an area because they were not born there. Africans want to be allowed to own land in places where they work, and not to be obliged to live in rented houses, which they can never call their own. Africans want to be part of the general population, and not confined to living in their own ghettos.

CHECKPOINT

Notice that all of the above sentences begin with the phrase "Africans want …" What effect does this have on you, the reader?

African men want to have their wives and children to live with them where they work, and not be forced into an unnatural existence in men's hostels. African women want to be with their menfolk and not be left permanently widowed in the Reserves. Africans want to be allowed out after eleven o'clock at night and not to be confined to their rooms like little children. Africans want to be allowed to travel in their own country and to seek work where they want to and not where the Labor Bureau tells them to. Africans want a just share in the whole of South Africa; they want security and a stake in society …

During my lifetime I have dedicated myself to this struggle of the African

---

endorsed: *recommended*
ghettos: *parts of a city occupied by minority groups*
Reserves: *segregated living areas*

people. I have fought against white domination, and I have fought against black domination. I have cherished the ideal of a democratic and free society in which all persons live together in harmony and with equal opportunities. It is an ideal, which I hope to live for and to achieve. But if needs be, it is an ideal for which I am prepared to die."

If Nelson Mandela was a threat to white South Africans as a saboteur, he was even more dangerous as a symbolic figure in prison. He came to represent for black South Africans all of the injustices that they had suffered, and they sought help to free Mandela from prison. He became such a rallying cry for his people that the government offered to release him from prison in 1985 if he renounced militant action, but he refused.

Not until 1990, as a result of mounting pressure from the African National Congress, was Nelson Mandela released from prison by the country's president, F. W. de Klerk. After sharing the Nobel Peace Prize with de Klerk in 1993, Mandela became the first black president of the country the following year. Since his retirement from office in 1999, Nelson Mandela has campaigned for human rights organizations and has been honored by the leaders of many nations for his courage and commitment to social justice issues.

Former political prisoner Nelson Mandela campaigns for the presidency of South Africa. Supporters cheer from the top of a billboard, 1994.

WEB CONNECTIONS

Using the Internet, find three ways in which Nelson Mandela continued to work, while in prison, for better conditions for black South Africans.

wrap up

1. Make a list of five phrases or sentences from Nelson Mandela's speech that show black South Africans were not treated equally. Share your list with a partner.

2. Imagine that it is 1990 and the South African government has just decided to release Nelson Mandela. In a small group, create a news report announcing this decision on national television. Act out your report in front of the class.

Jack Ruby (1963)

IT'S NOVEMBER 22, 1963, AND PRESIDENT JOHN F. KENNEDY IS GREETING THE PEOPLE OF DALLAS IN HIS PRESIDENTIAL MOTORCADE.

WELCOME TO DALLAS, MR. PRESIDENT!

WE LOVE YOU!!

warm up

Do you think that a judge should consider a murder victim's character when sentencing his or her murderer? Share your thoughts with a small group.

AS HE MAKES HIS WAY INTO DEALEY PLAZA HE'S UNAWARE OF WHAT'S WAITING FOR HIM ON THE SIXTH FLOOR OF THE TEXAS SCHOOL BOOK DEPOSITORY.

AN ASSASSIN, BELIEVED TO BE LEE HARVEY OSWALD, IS PREPARING TO FIRE THREE BULLETS THAT WILL FOREVER CHANGE AMERICA.

LIGHTS OUT, MR. KENNEDY...

BLAM! BLAM! BLAM!

Pencils: JEFF ALWARD Ink Finishes/colors: SANDY CARRUTHERS

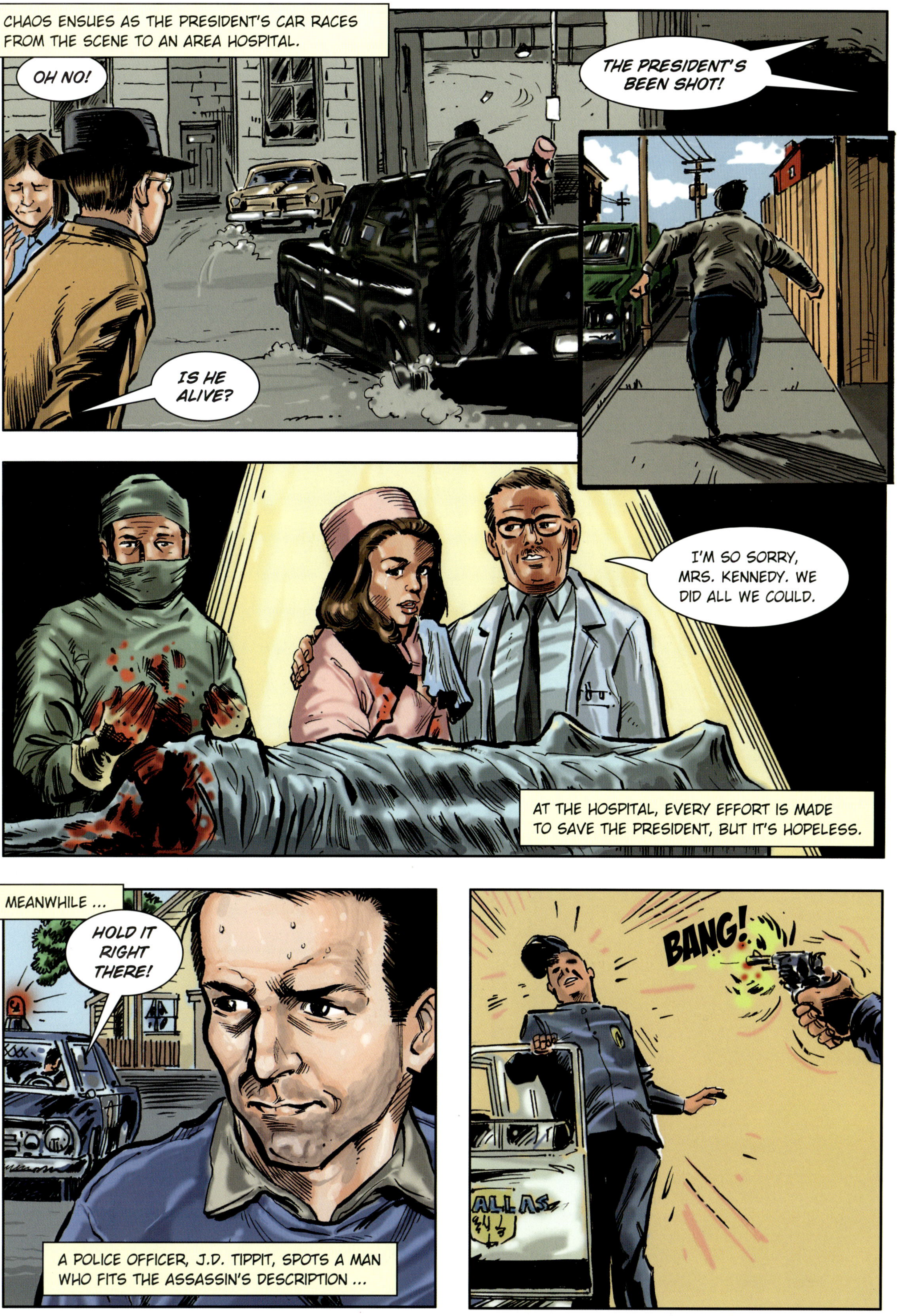

wrap up

1. Create a flow chart showing events from the assassination of President John F. Kennedy to the death of Ruby.

2. Go to the library and obtain the official findings of the Warren Commission about the motive for the assassination and who was responsible for it. Then, on the Internet, locate the many "conspiracy theories" that have sprung up since then. Share your findings on these theories with the class. Take a poll — which theory is closest to the truth?

FROM HEIRESS TO TERRORIST

PATTY HEARST (1976)

This photograph released by the FBI shows Patty Hearst with a machine gun, standing in front of a symbol of the Symbionese Liberation Army.

KIDNAPPED
BRAINWASHED
BEATEN
TRAUMATIZED

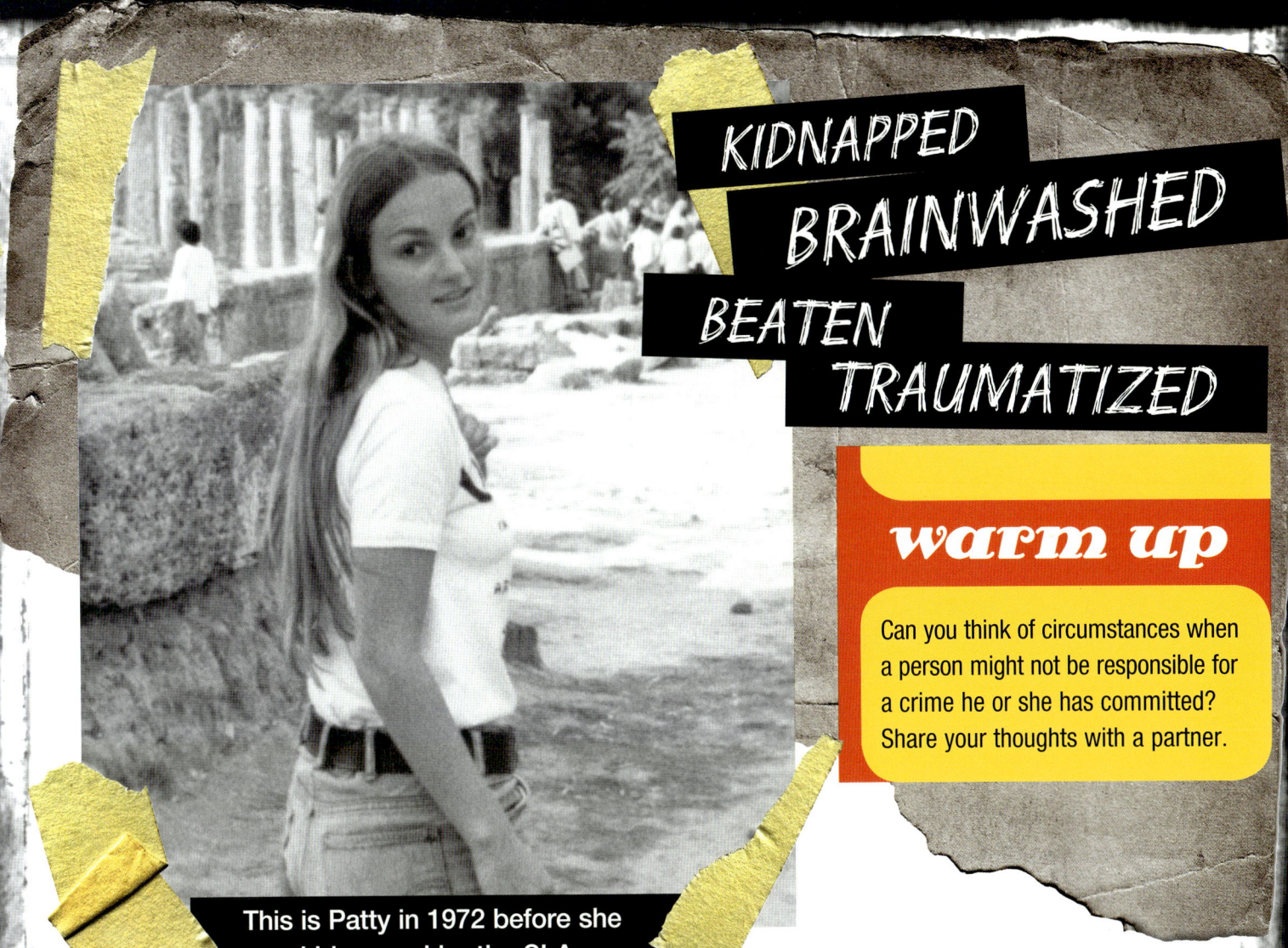

This is Patty in 1972 before she was kidnapped by the SLA.

warm up

Can you think of circumstances when a person might not be responsible for a crime he or she has committed? Share your thoughts with a partner.

You might think that in a book of famous trials, a case involving a bank robbery would not be spectacular enough to earn a place. But what if the defendant was the granddaughter of the most powerful newspaper publisher in the world, and what if she had been kidnapped by a group that brainwashed her into joining it to fight against people like her own family? This is exactly what happened to Patty Hearst on February 4, 1974.

A group calling itself the Symbionese Liberation Army (SLA) kidnapped Patty from her apartment. During the next two months, she was kept in a series of closets and only allowed out to use the toilet and to bathe. She was repeatedly yelled at, sexually assaulted, and traumatized, but sometimes she was treated with apparent kindness.

CHECKPOINT

What effect might these different treatments have on a person?

Her kidnappers, led by a man calling himself Cinque, also shouted slogans at her calling her and her family rich, white pigs who were oppressing the poor. She was brainwashed into believing that her family did not care about her. Imagine her family's shock when, on April 3, 1974, a tape was delivered that contained the voice of Patty Hearst saying that she had decided to join the SLA and had taken the name "Tania."

traumatized: *put in distressing situations*

Accompanied by marshals, Patty leaves a federal building after court proceedings.

Twelve days later, a video camera picked her up as she and the members of the SLA robbed the Hibernia Bank in San Francisco. She was now considered a fugitive and was pursued for the next year, during which time she participated in a couple of additional robberies. Police finally captured her on September 18, 1975. She was put on trial but it is generally considered to be one of the most mishandled trials of the 20th century for the following reasons:

The prosecutor was too eager to convict her.
- The chief prosecutor did not believe that Patty had been brainwashed. He felt, instead, that she had participated willingly and was thus nothing more than a common criminal.

CHECKPOINT
Why might he have felt this way?

Patty's defense team was ineffective.
- Her chief lawyer was the great criminal defense attorney, F. Lee Bailey, but his strategy in this case backfired. Bailey was known for his ability to confuse a jury so that they would refuse to convict his clients. This time, when the jury members got confused, they clung to the one thing they were sure of: Patty Hearst helped rob a bank.

The judge was incompetent.
- Judge Oliver Carter publicly expressed his opinion about the case in interviews with national newspapers before the trial, and made false claims about how well he knew the Hearst family. Both of these actions are strictly against the rules when serving as a judge on a case.

The public demanded that Patty not get preferential treatment.
- Because Patty was from a wealthy family, she was convicted in the court of public opinion before the jury convicted

---

fugitive: *wanted criminal*   preferential: *special*

CHECKPOINT

Why might Patty Hearst's wealth have made people believe she was guilty?

her. She was sentenced to 35 years in prison. This was later reduced to seven years. In a subsequent trial for another bank robbery, the judge was convinced that Patty's wealth had prevented her from getting a fair trial and he refused to give her additional jail time. Instead, he sentenced her to five years probation.

Patty did not actually have to go to prison until 1978 because she had appealed her case. In 1979, President Jimmy Carter commuted her sentence after a long campaign by a number of people who felt that she had been unfairly convicted. President Bill Clinton eventually pardoned Patty Hearst in 2001.

commuted: *changed the penalty to a less severe form*

Patty's grandfather, William Randolph Hearst, was a newspaper magnate and the subject of Orson Welles' great film masterpiece, *Citizen Kane*.

Patty Hearst has been featured in several films, including *Cry-Baby*, *Cecil B. DeMented*, and *Serial Mom*.

WEB CONNECTIONS

Using the Internet, find out what Patty Hearst's life has been like in the last 10 years. Share your findings with the class.

STOCKHOLM SYNDROME

Most experts on the Patty Hearst case believe that during her kidnapping she developed what is known as the Stockholm Syndrome. This syndrome occurs when persons held against their will begin to develop a sympathetic relationship with their kidnappers. The term comes from a situation that developed during a six-day bank robbery turned hostage situation in Sweden in 1973.

In the Stockholm bank robbery, the hostages not only attempted to defend the robbers during the crisis, but they did not seem to have an interest in seeing them prosecuted afterward.

CHECKPOINT

Why might the victims have reacted this way?

Patty Hearst later admitted that identifying with her captors was a way to ensure her survival. When she was asked to join the SLA, she realized that it was not a choice between joining them or being freed, but it was between joining them or being killed.

syndrome: *a group of symptoms that are characteristic of a specific disorder*
identifying: *connecting emotionally*

wrap up

1. Write a four-line chorus for a song about the life of Patty Hearst. You might want to look up songs like "Davy Crockett" or "Pinball Wizard" as examples.

2. "When it comes to being put on trial in the court of public opinion, it does not pay to be rich." In a small group discussion, agree or disagree with this statement. Explain your opinion in a short paragraph.

TO WHOM IT MAY CONCERN

O.J. Simpson in a slow-speed chase with police after being charged with two counts of murder

O.J. SIMPSON (1995)

warm up

Should a person's emotional reaction upon being charged with a crime be used as evidence against him or her? Share your opinion with the rest of the class.

CHECKPOINT

Have you begun to form an opinion about Simpson's guilt or innocence at this point?

CHECKPOINT

How might a suicide note be an indication of a person's guilt or innocence?

The O.J. Simpson trial was remarkable for many reasons, including the fact that many people had decided on the defendant's guilt or innocence long before the trial even began. Simpson, a star running back for the Buffalo Bills, was charged with murdering his ex-wife, Nicole Brown Simpson, and an acquaintance, Ronald Goldman, on June 12, 1994. There was a great deal of evidence against him: blood, hair, and fibers that connected Simpson with the crime scene, as well as a pair of matching gloves, one found at the crime scene and one found at his residence.

Simpson assembled a dream team of lawyers that used their experience to *outmaneuver* the prosecution on a number of occasions. After an eight-month trial, the jury found Simpson "not guilty" on both murder counts.

Below is an excerpt from what was known as Simpson's "suicide letter," written just five days after the murders. A friend read it on national television when Simpson fled from police in a white Ford Bronco driven by another friend who reported to police that O.J. was threatening to kill himself. Some people think that the suicide note is evidence of Simpson's guilt, while others think the opposite. What do you think?

outmaneuver: outsmart

To whom it may concern:

First, everyone understand I have nothing to do with Nicole's murder. I loved her, always have and always will. If we had a problem, it's because I loved her so much …

Despite our love we were different, and that's why we mutually agreed to go our separate ways. It was tough splitting for a second time, but we both knew it was for the best.

Inside I had no doubt that in the future we would be close as friends or more. Unlike what has been written in the press, Nicole and I had a great relationship for most of our lives together. Like all long-term relationships, we had a few downs and ups. I took the heat New Year's 1989 because that's what I was supposed to do. I did not plead no contest for any other reason but to protect our privacy and was advised it would end the press hype.

I don't want to **belabor** knocking the press, but I can't believe what is being said. Most of it is totally made up. I know you have a job to do, but as a last wish, please, please, please, leave my children in peace. Their lives will be tough enough …

I think of my life and feel I've done most of the right things. Whatever the outcome, people will look and point. I can't take that. I can't subject my children to that. This way they can move on and go on with their lives. Please, if I've done anything worthwhile in my life. Let my kids live in peace from you (the press).

I've had a good life. I'm proud of how I lived. My mama taught me to do unto others. I treated people the way I wanted to be treated. I've always tried to be up and helpful so why is this happening? I'm sorry for the Goldman family. I know how much it hurts.

Nicole and I had a good life together. All this press talk about a rocky relationship was no more than what every long-term relationship experiences. All her friends will confirm that I have been totally loving and understanding of what she's been going through. At times I have felt like a battered husband or boyfriend but I loved her, make that clear to everyone. And I would take whatever it took to make it work.

Don't feel sorry for me. I've had a great life, great friends. Please think of the real O.J. and not this lost person.

Thanks for making my life special. I hope I helped yours.

Peace and love,  O.J.

---

belabor: *dwell on*

FYI

Although Simpson was found "not guilty" in the criminal trial, a subsequent civil trial found him legally responsible for the deaths of Nicole Brown Simpson and Ronald Goldman. The Brown family received $12.5 million in damages and the Goldman family was awarded $21 million.

CHECKPOINT

Think of reasons why Simpson's accusation of the press might be fair or unfair.

wrap up

1. With a partner, look for evidence in Simpson's letter that you feel points to either his guilt or innocence, and create two separate lists of evidence.

2. In a small group, discuss some recent criminal cases where the press has affected how you feel about the guilt or innocence of the defendants.

WHEN CHI

warm up

What do you think is worse, a violent crime committed by a child or a violent crime committed against a child? Share your opinions with a partner.

CHECKPOINT
Think of other examples where someone's minor crimes have led to those with far more serious consequences.

CHECKPOINT
What do you think you might have done in this situation?

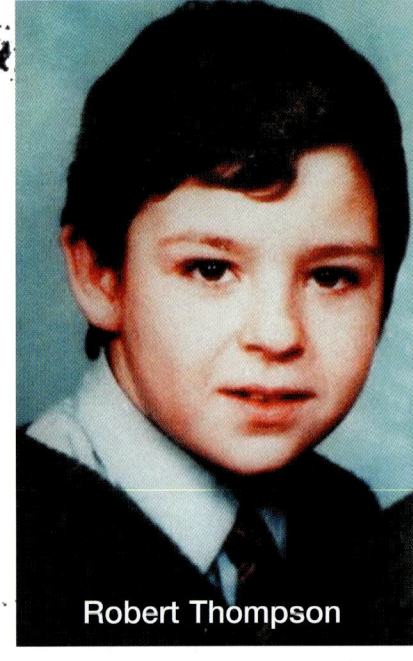
Robert Thompson

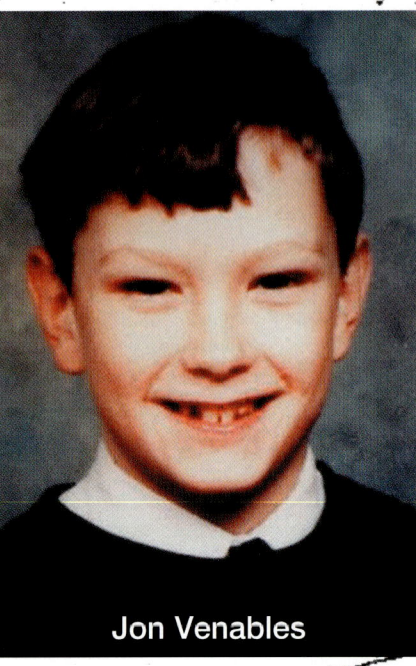
Jon Venables

On February 12, 1993, two-year-old James Bulger disappeared from the New Strand shopping center in Bootle, Merseyside, England. Later his body was found about two miles away on railway tracks. When police arrested two 10-year-old boys in connection with the crime, people around the world were shocked.

Jon Venables and Robert Thompson were friends who skipped school, stole candy from stores, and hung out together. But their petty crimes turned into something far more terrible than anyone could have expected. While little James was in the shopping mall with his mother, the two older boys lured him away. Video cameras showed Venables and Thompson leading the toddler out of the mall.

Venables and Thompson beat James. Several passersby asked the two older boys what they were doing with the frightened toddler; but no one took him away from his would-be murderers.

The case caused a sensation in Britain, with parents frightened that their children were no longer safe from other children.

petty: *minor*

...LDREN KILL

JON VENABLES AND ROBERT THOMPSON (1993)

CCTV image showing James Bulger being led away by one of his abductors

Venables and Thompson were put on trial as adults. They did not fully understand what was happening. Throughout the trial, the boys could be seen fiddling with paper or sucking their thumbs. Some people felt the boys should be imprisoned for life, or even put to death, for their crimes. Others felt they had not received a fair trial.

The boys were sentenced to serve eight years and then 10 years on appeal. When it was bumped up to 15, this was overturned on appeal, and the boys were released in 2001, on what is called "a life license."

> **CHECKPOINT**
> Are you surprised by the people's reactions?

In 1999, the European Court on Human Rights ruled that Venables and Thompson had not received a fair trial and put pressure on the British courts to review their sentences.

CHECKPOINT

Notice how passionate these two people are about this case.

wrap up

1. In a group, discuss what you think an appropriate punishment would be for children who commit first-degree murder.

2. Write a letter to the parole board that decided to release Jon Venables and Robert Thompson and express your support for, or disapproval of, its decision.

WEB CONNECTIONS

Use the Internet to find out why some people believe that the trial of Venables and Thompson was unfair. With a partner, briefly summarize the opinions of three people. Indicate the source of each of your pieces.

The decision to release the boys after only eight years aroused strong emotional reactions from the public, with people for and against the decision. Two typical opposing views were presented on the BBC news program *Head to Head*.

Lyn Costello, representing the group Mothers Against Murder and Aggression, stated: "We don't believe eight years is punishment. Of course we believe in rehabilitation, but what about punishment?"

Mark Leech, from the ex-offenders charity, Unlock, expressed the opposite view: "Nothing that anyone can do will bring James Bulger back; we should allow them [Venables and Thompson] now to get on with their lives."

The funeral of James Bulger in Liverpool

ERIN BROCKOVICH (1993-94)

The year was 1987 and Pacific Gas and Electric had just announced that it had found the cancer-causing element chromium-6 in an area of the Mohave Desert near one of their gas compressor stations in Hinkley, California. Chromium-6 is a carcinogenic chemical that can cause very serious health problems, especially in the lungs. Pacific Gas and Electric stated that things were not as bad as they seemed. The company assured the locals that all was well or would be made well through a clean-up program. However, it advised residents to avoid using well water.

They continued to assure the public that they were not in any serious danger. However, there were three very serious problems with this. Many people and animals in the area were either sick — especially with respiratory ailments — or had died. Secondly, records showed that Pacific Gas and Electric had known about the chromium-6 problem since 1965 and had not told anyone about it. Now

carcinogenic: *cancer-causing*
ailments: *illnesses*

warm up

What do the terms "civil trial" and "criminal trial" mean to you? Share your thoughts with the rest of the class.

CHECKPOINT

Why would the company try to put the public's mind at ease?

Erin Brockovich in her home in Agoura Hills, California, March 24, 2000

FYI

Anderson v. Pacific Gas and Electric is known as a class action lawsuit in which many people band together to sue a major company or government agency.

Today, Ms. Brockovich continues to work as a lawyer's assistant but spends her off-hours lecturing on the effects of toxic dumping.

CONFIDENTIAL INFORMATION ENCLOSED

the soil and ground water contamination was being reported as a new discovery. When the company began buying up and leveling property around the plant, a law firm employee, Erin Brockovich, discovered that the company had an unusual interest in the medical records of those whose properties it was buying. They appeared to be getting rid of people who might take legal action and then destroying the evidence of contamination.

CHECKPOINT
What laws do you think the company was breaking by doing this?

What Erin Brockovich exposed was a terrible web of lies that would result in a civil trial in 1993/94 — Anderson v. Pacific Gas and Electric — with dozens, and eventually hundreds, of complainants and a lawsuit that asked for hundreds of millions of dollars in damages. The case was important because it showed that sometimes the little guy, and not the big company, wins.

Erin Brockovich and her boss, Ed Masry, put in the time and effort to examine countless pages of documents in order to get at the truth about the corrupt and irresponsible business practices of a major company. When the court decision came down, they won a major victory. The judgment was in favor of the plaintiffs, and Pacific Gas and Electric was forced to pay $333 million in damages.

The story behind this famous trial became so well known that, in 2000, it was turned into a major film, *Erin Brockovich*, starring Julia Roberts and Albert Finney. The film was a hit and Julia Roberts, inspired by the courage and dedication of Erin Brockovich, won the Academy Award for Best Actress.

contamination: *pollution*
plaintiffs: *persons who initiate lawsuits*

Actress Julia Roberts portrays Erin Brockovich, a law clerk who fights for the rights of the underdog.

wrap up

1. Write a news report based on the information in this article. Create a headline, a lead sentence, and roughly 100 words of text that contain a minimum of three details from the article.

2. With a partner, create a mock interview in which one of you composes three questions to ask Erin Brockovich, and the other prepares three answers that she might give. Act out your interview for the class.

WEB CONNECTIONS

With a partner, search the Internet to find other films that feature civil or class action lawsuits. Find a synopsis of one of these films and share with the class any similarities it has with the story of Erin Brockovich.

ACKNOWLEDGMENTS

The publisher gratefully acknowledges the following for permission to reprint copyrighted material in this book.

Every reasonable effort has been made to trace the owners of copyrighted material and to make due acknowledgment. Any errors or omissions drawn to our attention will be gladly rectified in future editions.

Janice Tibbetts: "Truscott Hopes for Final Exoneration" from *Calgary Herald*, p. A17, CanWest News Service, 15 April 2004. Permission courtesy of CanWest News.